Celebrity Biographies

America Ferrera

LATINA SUPERSTAR

SHEILA ANDERSON

E Enslow Publishers, Inc.

40 Industrial Road
Box 398
Berkeley Heights, NJ 07922
USA
http://www.enslow.com

Library of Congress Cataloging-in-Publication Data
Anderson, Sheila.
  America Ferrera : Latina superstar / Sheila Anderson.
    p. cm. — (Hot celebrity biographies)
  Includes bibliographical references and index.
  Summary: "Read about America Ferrera's life—from her first movie to the star of a hit tv show. Find out how she spends her free time, and what she wants to do in the future"—Provided by publisher.
  ISBN-13: 978-0-7660-3210-1
  ISBN-10: 0-7660-3210-8
  1. Ferrera, America, 1984—Juvenile literature. 2. Actors—United States—Biography—Juvenile literature. I. Title.
  PN2287.F423A53 2009
  791.4302'8092—dc22
  [B]
                                2008026463

Paperback ISBN-13: 978-0-7660-3625-3
Paperback ISBN-10: 0-7660-3625-1

Printed in the United States of America

10 9 8 7 6 5 4 3 2 1

To our readers: We have done our best to make sure all Internet Addresses in this book were active and appropriate when we went to press. However, the author and the publisher have no control over and assume no liability for the material available on those Internet sites or on other Web sites they may link to. Any comments or suggestions can be sent by e-mail to comments@enslow.com or to the address on the back cover.

 Enslow Publishers, Inc., is committed to printing our books on recycled paper. The paper in every book contains 10% to 30% post-consumer waste (PCW). The cover board on the outside of each book contains 100% PCW. Our goal is to do our part to help young people and the environment too!

Photographs: Lisa Rose/AP Images, 1; Gus Ruelas/AP Images, 4; Peter Kramer/AP Images, 7; Avik Gilboa/WireImage/ Getty Images, 8; Reed Saxon/AP Images, 9, 31; Chris Pizzello/AP Images, 11, 23, 34; Matt Sayles/AP Images, 12, 24, 39; Tammie Arroyo/AP Images, 15; Stefano Paltera/AP Images, 16; Luis Martinez/AP Images, 17; Stephen Chernin/AP Images, 20, 33; Mark Mainz/Getty Images, 25; Dan Steinberg/AP Images, 27; Kristie Bull/Graylock.com/AP Images, 28; Nick Ut/AP Images, 32; Ric Francis/AP Images, 37; AP Images, 41

Cover photo: America Ferrera arrives for the Emmy Awards on September 21, 2008.
Lisa Rose/AP Images.

Contents

America the Beautiful

"And the winner is . . . America Ferrera!"

"Yeah! Woo-hoo!" the crowd roared. People sprang to their feet in noisy applause. A broad smile spread across the actress's face. She glowed as she walked gracefully to the stage. Her acceptance speech was genuine, sincere, and grateful.

Who is this young star, and what was the occasion? She is America Ferrera, and this was the scene at the 2007 Emmy Awards. She won the title of Best Actress in a Comedy Series for her role as Betty Suarez on the hit television show *Ugly Betty*.

But ugly does not describe this pretty, graceful actress. She hardly looks out of place as she walks the red carpet in a beautiful evening gown. And when she opens her mouth, watch out! America is one down-to-earth person, making her that much more attractive.

◀ *America Ferrera, pictured in 2007, hopes to be a positive role model for Latina girls.*

AMERICA FERRERA

AMERICA AT A GLANCE

Nickname: Georgina

Childhood ambition: To be a lawyer

Education: University of Southern California, Los Angeles, CA

Personal style: "Princess Diana with a little Beyoncé mixed in"

If she weren't an actress: She would be a teacher.

WHO IS AMERICA FERRERA?

In addition to being a successful actress at a young age, America Ferrera is a sister, a daughter, a girlfriend, a dog owner, a bilingual Latina, and a college graduate.

America Georgina Ferrera was born on April 18, 1984, in Los Angeles, California. Her family often calls her Georgina.

America's parents immigrated to the United States from Honduras years before she was born. Her siblings include an older brother and four older sisters.

America's parents divorced when she was seven years old. After they split up, her father moved back to Honduras. America has not seen him since. Her mother raised America and her siblings by herself in Woodland Hills, California. America's mother worked as the supervisor in charge of housekeeping services for a large hotel. Raising six children on her own was hard work.

▲ *Despite her success and fame, America Ferrera is known for her down-to-earth personality.*

America's mother stressed to her children the importance of studying hard and getting a good education. Her children listened to her. All six earned college degrees. America's mother can be proud of her children's accomplishments.

CAUGHT BETWEEN WORLDS

America was caught between two worlds when she was growing up. Because she was Latina, people sometimes asked her if she was Latin or American. But America lived in a mostly white neighborhood, and she identified with her

▲ *America Ferrera's mother* (right) *encouraged her and her siblings to go to college.*

white peers. Despite this, people who did not know her saw her as a Latina.

America says she never really thought of herself as a Latina until she started trying out for acting roles. Then she began to understand some of the struggles faced by many Latin Americans. These are the same struggles faced by many of the characters America has played in films and on television.

America understands the pressure that U.S. culture places on young people, especially young women. Those expectations sometimes differ from traditional Latin values. For instance, family is very important to many Latinos. This means that members of a family are expected to support each other in any way they can. This is true even if it means that they must give up their personal dreams to do so.

TOTALLY QUOTABLE

On her mom not wanting her to act: "Acting was not something that they came to this country to have me do."

On coming from a big family: "I never had a ton of friends. I always had two or three, but when you have four sisters and a brother all a year apart, you don't really need anyone else to play with."

On her appearance: "I never wanted to be a model. I set out to tell stories."

▲ America Ferrera holds the Screen Actors Guild award she won in 2007.

America makes an effort to be a positive role model for Latina girls. She tries to show them that they can reach their goals if they work hard and follow their hearts. They may face unfair treatment at times because of their ethnic groups. But America wants them to know that they should be proud of who they are.

CURVY AND PROUD

Regardless of her family or background, America says that weight has always been an issue for her. Girls in the United States face pressure from society to be thin. They see so many images of skinny models in magazines and ads. Despite these pressures, Ferrera maintains a healthy weight.

America embraces her curvy figure—something that is celebrated in Latin America. Latin society does not link thin with beautiful like American society does. "I think Hispanic women are beautiful with their curves," she says. Ferrera encourages all girls, not just Latinas, to be comfortable with their bodies and to accept themselves as they are.

America Ferrera, pictured at the Screen Actors Guild Awards in 2008, ▶ has a very healthy body image.

Rising Star

When she was growing up, America was a good student. She understood the importance of education. She applied herself in school just as her mother expected. She graduated from high school with an A average. After high school, America's mother wanted her to go to college. She was not excited about America's dream of becoming an actress.

But America knew from the time she was a little girl that she wanted to be an actress when she grew up. She dreamed of being a star. Backstage at the 2007 Primetime Emmys, America said, "This is all I ever wanted to do since I was about five."

PAYING HER DUES
When America was seven years old, she took part in her school's production of Shakespeare's play *Hamlet*. From that point forward, she was hooked on acting.

◀ *America Ferrera dreamed of being an actress from the time she was a little girl.*

When America was eight years old, she began acting in Los Angeles community theater. She continued to act in school and community theater productions throughout her school years.

As a teenager, America worked as a waitress to earn money so that she could take acting classes. Her mother encouraged her to earn her own way. She helped America get a job in a restaurant. This way, America could pay for her own acting classes and the photographs that she needed taken to get acting jobs.

America's mother was busy working and taking care of her large family. So, she was not always available to drive America to acting auditions. When America began auditioning for acting jobs, she had to take the bus to her auditions.

BREAKING THROUGH

When Ferrera was sixteen years old, she signed on with a small talent agency. She tried out for television ads and other acting jobs. And she quickly got her first big acting role. At age seventeen, Ferrera was cast in the Disney television movie *Gotta Kick It Up!* In the movie, Ferrera's character is part of a middle school's struggling dance team. The girls on

THE FUTURE SHINES BRIGHT

When America Ferrera landed her role in *Gotta Kick It Up!*, she joked, "Disney Channel today, Oscars tomorrow!" Ferrera has won many awards for her work, including an Emmy, a Golden Globe, and a Screen Actors Guild Award.

▶ *America Ferrera's first big role was in* Gotta Kick It Up!

the team have to work together to prove that they have what it takes to win a dance competition.

Ferrera was very excited when she landed this role because it sounded like so much fun. "I love to dance, so I couldn't

▲ *The cast of* The Sisterhood of the Traveling Pants *poses for a photo.*

believe I was getting paid to just dance all day!" she said. Who wouldn't love a job like that?

Her next big break came when Ferrera was eighteen years old. She had just graduated from El Camino Real High School. She got the starring role in the movie *Real Women Have Curves*. This was her first feature film. In the movie, Ferrera's character is caught between two worlds. Her Latino parents want her to work to help support the family. Her own wish is to go to college. Like *Gotta Kick It Up!*, this movie looks at the roles of women and Hispanics in the United States. It highlights issues that are important to Ferrera.

Her energetic performance in this role earned Ferrera nominations for a number of awards. She was nominated for a Spirit Award for Best Debut Performance and a Young Artist Award for Best Performance by a Leading Young Actress. Her performance in this role also won Ferrera a Jury Award for Best Actress at the Sundance Film Festival.

After *Real Women Have Curves*, Ferrera played various roles in plays, film, and on television. The work ranged from short-term roles on shows like *CSI: Crime Scene Investigation* to starring roles in hit movies like *The Sisterhood of the Traveling Pants*. The sequel came out in August 2008.

Sisterhood tells the story of four young friends who are being pulled in different directions one summer. To stay in touch, they pass around a pair of jeans that, in spite of their different sizes and shapes, magically seems to fit all of them. Ferrera played Carmen, a Latina teen

▶ The *Sisterhood cast arrives at the Kids' Choice Awards.*

AMERICA FERRERA'S CREDITS

Movies

Real Women Have Curves (2002)

Darkness Minus Twelve (2004)

The Sisterhood of the Traveling Pants (2005)

Lords of Dogtown (2005)

How the Garcia Girls Spent Their Summer (2005)

Steel City (2006)

Towards Darkness (2007)

Under the Same Moon (2007)

The Sisterhood of the Traveling Pants 2 (2008)

Television

Touched By An Angel (2002)

Gotta Kick It Up! (2002)

CSI: Crime Scene Investigation (2004)

Plainsong (2004)

Ugly Betty (2006)

Theater

The Have Little (2002)

Dog Sees God: Confessions of a Teenage Blockhead (2006)

who lives with her Puerto Rican single mother. She is going to spend the summer with her white father.

When she arrives, she's surprised to find her father is engaged to another woman who has two children of her own. Carmen is disappointed not to have her father to herself and struggles to fit in with his new family.

Another one of her movies takes on much more serious subject matter. The Spanish-language movie *Towards Darkness* tells the story of a kidnapping in Colombia. Although Ferrera is already bilingual because of her Honduran parents, she had to study up on her Spanish for the role. She watched other Spanish-language movies and took lessons to get the Colombian accent right. Since the movie was filmed in Panama, her other challenge was working in the heat. She was so uncomfortable that she didn't even wear makeup in the film.

Ferrera has said she hopes the movie will draw attention to the large number of kidnappings happening in Colombia. "The rate in Colombia is awful," she said. "More than one person a day is kidnapped there."

In 2004, Ferrera acted in the television pilot *$5.15/Hour,* which was not picked up by a network. Despite this, it helped get her feet wet in the arena of TV-series acting. But Ferrera's rocket ship toward stardom took off when she landed the lead role on the hit television comedy *Ugly Betty* in 2006.

Becoming "Ugly Betty"

America Ferrera is anything but ugly in real life. Still, she plays the severely style-challenged character Betty Suarez on the funny TV hit *Ugly Betty*. The show is based on a Colombian soap opera with a similar name.

Betty is a simple-looking young woman in a glitzy career where she just doesn't fit in. She is the assistant to the editor of a high-fashion magazine. Her coworkers strut by in high heels and pencil skirts. But Betty stumbles down the company's halls in sweater vests and shapeless dresses. All the while, she is attempting to dislodge bits of lunch from her braces.

But there's more to Betty than the frumpy wardrobe, bushy eyebrows, braces, thick glasses, and styleless hairdo. Betty is a heartwarming character with intelligence and kindness. She sends the message to viewers that beauty really is only skin-deep. Despite her outward appearance, Betty is a caring, creative, competent person with a whole lot to offer.

◀ *America Ferrera hopes* Ugly Betty *gives people more than just laughs. She wants to get them thinking.*

UGLY BETTY'S ROOTS

Ugly Betty is based on a Colombian soap opera called *Yo Soy Betty La Fea*. The original tells the story of an unattractive but capable woman who goes to work for a fashion design company. She faces similar obstacles to the U.S. version, but eventually gets promoted, gets dates, and gets a makeover.

Producers around the world have discovered the wide appeal of the unattractive but likable character—realizing that not every television star has to look like a model to be successful. More than a dozen versions of the popular show have been made in other countries, including Israel, India, Turkey, Germany, Russia, Mexico, Spain, Greece, and Portugal.

BORN TO BE BETTY

Ferrera loves playing the role of Betty. As Betty, she says, she feels extremely confident—even more so than she does as her naturally beautiful self!

"You know, when I'm in character and I'm wearing Betty's costume, I never feel more confident, more beautiful, and more pretty on the inside," Ferrera has said. "I wish that I, one day, as America, could feel the way that I feel when I'm Betty. When I'm Betty, there's a light that shines from the inside."

It's true. No matter what obstacles she faces, "Ugly Betty" approaches them head-on with an incredible can-do attitude. And she's not only determined—she's smart.

▲ *America Ferrera attends a DVD release party for* Ugly Betty.

Ferrera has said about Betty, "When you watch her, when you actually listen to what she says and see how smart she is, you realize she is beautiful." Betty is brilliant. She's awesome. She's inspiring. (Not unlike the actress playing her!)

But *Ugly Betty* is about more than just beauty and fashion. In addition to being made fun of by her coworkers, Betty deals with difficult situations in her home life. At home, she is a caretaker. She is constantly looking after her unhealthy father and trying to keep the family together and functional. The family also faces legal issues that are very real for many Hispanics.

THE "BETTIFICATION" OF AMERICA FERRERA

Even though she plays the character "Ugly Betty," hardly anyone would call America Ferrera ugly. Actually, it takes a lot of time and effort to make the pretty young actress look so plain. Ferrera started calling the process "Bettification." The makeup artist uses dark eyeliner to create Betty's bushy brows. The hair department created a wig that's supposed to look like Betty just showers and goes each morning—no styling products or hair dryer involved.

And of course, a lot of thought has gone into Betty's unusual fashion taste. Her typical work outfit consists of a blouse, vest, and skirt. She once wore a butterfly outfit on Halloween and a tacky old prom dress to a four-star restaurant. Betty's accessories include chunky reading glasses and her braces—actually a removable plastic piece that Ferrera can take off when she's not filming.

▲ *America Ferrera displays the Emmy she won for her work on* Ugly Betty *in 2007.*

▲ *The cast of* Ugly Betty *is presented with a portrait of the title character backstage at the Golden Globes in 2007.*

MORE THAN JUST LAUGHS

Ferrera feels that being an actress is about more than just providing people with entertainment. She wants people to be affected by what they see and hear on *Ugly Betty*. She wants them to think a little and to learn about other ways of life. "It feels good to be a part of a show that means more to people than just entertainment, and which confronts a lot of issues, like the portrayal of a Latin family with a father struggling for citizenship," she has said.

Ugly Betty has its funny side and its serious side. But the show does not make broad statements about Latinos or Latin families. Ferrera told *USA Today*, "It's not about stereotypes. They're not hitting piñatas every weekend. More important than having Latinos on TV is having a representation of the variations of what a Latino is."

Ferrera got the role of Betty after meeting Salma Hayek on the set of *The Oprah Winfrey Show*. Hayek is one of *Ugly Betty's* executive producers. Hayek said of Ferrera, "I knew the minute that I saw her that she was a superstar."

In 2007, Ferrera won an Emmy for her role in *Ugly Betty*. In her acceptance speech, Ferrera explained how grateful she was to have the role. She said she appreciates being on the show because it is not only entertaining, but also meaningful. The comedy has a message behind it. It makes you root for the underdog and appreciate what ordinary people have to offer, she explained. You become aware of the huge promise each person has. You just have to have the drive and courage to go for it—whatever your goals may be.

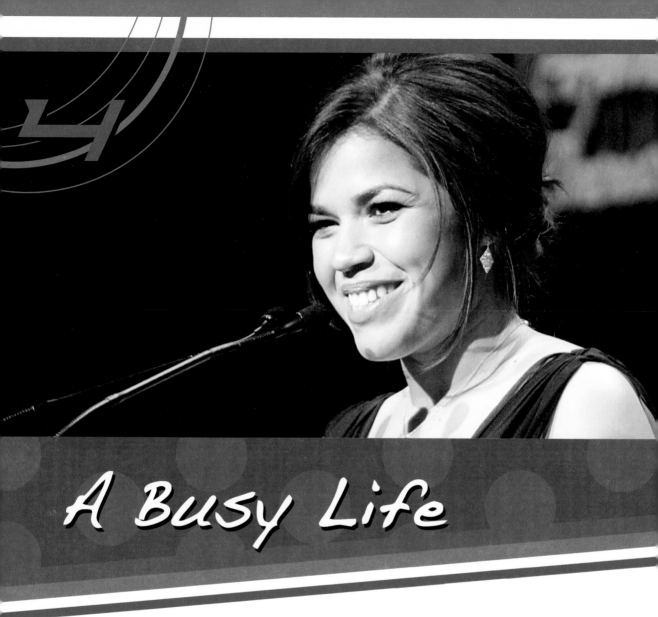

A Busy Life

Because of her packed acting schedule, Ferrera doesn't find much time to pursue other interests. Her rehearsal schedule for *Ugly Betty* sometimes requires her to work twelve hours a day! Sometimes the actors practice until the early morning hours.

▲ *America Ferrera speaks at the 2007 National Hispanic Media Coalition's Impact Awards.*

COVER GIRL

Ferrera has been featured on the cover of numerous magazines. You may have seen her face on *Disney Newsreel, TV Guide, TV Week,* or *Latina* in 2006, or on *Cosmo Girl, Glamour, Entertainment Weekly, W, Latina, Out,* or *PDTV* in 2007. In 2008, she graced the cover of *Seventeen*.

▶ *Magazines have taken an interest in Ferrera.*

When she is on break from *Ugly Betty,* Ferrera pursues other acting opportunities. Because she feels so strongly about acting, she does not feel like she is missing out on other activities. Acting is exactly what she wants to be doing.

And being so busy keeps her out of the kinds of trouble some young celebrities find themselves in. The party lifestyle is not for Ferrera.

MAKING TIME FOR SCHOOL

Despite her busy schedule, Ferrera has never forgotten the importance her mother placed on education. At the same time her acting career was blossoming, Ferrera was a student at the University of Southern California. She graduated from college in 2007 with a double major in theater and international relations. Now that's ambitious!

"Acting is something I knew I wanted to do long term," Ferrera said. "But not going to college was not an option. I think it probably helped me as an actress as well, because actresses need real-life experiences to draw from."

While she was a student at the University of Southern California, Ferrera met her longtime boyfriend, Ryan Piers Williams. The two started dating after Williams cast Ferrera in a student film he was directing. The couple has been inseparable ever since.

When not acting or spending time with Williams, Ferrera has pursued the production side of film. In 2007, she not only acted in but also produced the Colombian film

FERRERA'S FAVORITE CAUSES

Peace Games
An organization that helps children create a peaceful atmosphere in their schools through education and working together

Smiles for Success
A group that provides free dental care to women who have completed a workforce readiness program

Hillblazers
Hillary Clinton's youth outreach program

Towards Darkness. She hopes to do more movie production and eventually move into directing.

Ferrera is always looking for her next project and setting the bar higher and higher for herself. This is one of the reasons why she has been so successful in her acting career.

HELPING OUT
Ferrera has done her part to help other people and to have a positive effect on the world. In 2007, she performed in a variety show at the Henry Fonda Music Box Theater for the charity event "Hot In Hollywood." In addition to the celebrity performances, the event included an auction. It raised more than $200,000 for AIDS research and prevention.

Ferrera supports other charities as well. One is an organization called Peace Games. It teaches students how to create a safe and peaceful atmosphere in their schools through education and working together. Programs offered by Peace Games teach children to appreciate and value the people around them. They also teach students how to solve conflicts peacefully through communication and cooperation.

Another charity organization Ferrera supports is Smiles for Success. This group provides free dental care for women who have completed a workforce readiness program. These women want to leave welfare and enter the workforce.

▼ *America Ferrera and other cast members of* Ugly Betty *joined the picket lines during the Hollywood writers' strike in 2007.*

By fixing their teeth, the program improves both their smiles and their self-esteem. That can be key to getting a job that will help them support their families.

▲ *America Ferrera attends a young voter rally with actress Amber Tamblyn (left).*

Ferrera also has become involved in politics. For the 2008 election, she co-chaired Hillblazers, Hillary Clinton's youth outreach program. Ferrera also hoped to encourage women and Latinos to vote for Clinton in the 2008 presidential race, but Clinton did not become the Democratic nominee.

Leading up to the November election, Ferrera appeared in public service announcements for "Countdown to Youth Vote." The ad campaign encouraged voter turnout among multicultural youth.

SAVING THE PLANET, ONE LIGHT BULB AT A TIME

Ferrera is interested in helping the planet as well. This is one cause that benefits everyone. Ferrera's efforts to help the planet begin with driving a hybrid car. Hybrid cars are fueled by both gasoline and electricity. They use less fuel than other cars, and they pollute the air less. Ferrera uses energy-saving light bulbs instead of regular light bulbs in her home.

Ferrera feels that everyone, whether a regular teenager or a well-known celebrity, can help protect the planet in big and little ways. And she is happy to do her part.

▶ *Charity work is a big part of America Ferrera's life.*

Staying Down to Earth

A person with Ferrera's talent is sure to get some applause. The young actress has already gotten her share—from her fans, from the acting community, and even from Congress!

In addition to her Emmy, Ferrera received a Golden Globe in 2007 for Best Actress in a Comedy. Also in 2007, Ferrera won an acting award from the Screen Actors Guild. That same year, *TIME* magazine named her one of the top one hundred most influential people in the world! She also has been named Hispanic Woman of the Year by *Billboard* and *Hollywood Reporter,* and one of the fifteen most influential Hispanics in the United States by *People en Español*.

One of the biggest honors for Ferrera in 2007 might have been the recognition she received from Congress. Congresswoman Hilda L. Solis addressed Congress to praise Ferrera for changing the image of Latinos in the United States. "I rise today to congratulate America Ferrera for winning the Golden Globe for Best Actress in a Comedy for

◀ *America Ferrera arrives at the 2007 Emmy Awards. She has won many awards for her work on* Ugly Betty.

SINGING FERRERA'S PRAISES

Salma Hayek, executive producer of *Ugly Betty*: "She's one of the most charismatic people I've ever met. She's also authentic. That's a rare characteristic nowadays, and that's why people are falling in love with her."

Ben Silverman, *Ugly Betty* executive producer: "It doesn't matter what makeup or hair or clothing she has on, she's so real that she grabs you. She's a very connected human being, and that really empowers her as an actor."

her work in the ABC show *Ugly Betty*," Solis said. "Through her work, Ms. Ferrera is breaking down barriers for Latinos in prime-time television. I commend America and everyone in *Ugly Betty* for helping to break down stereotypes and provide a role model for young Latinas."

KEEPING IT REAL

Despite the many awards she has won, Ferrera is very down to earth. Of course she dresses up like any other Hollywood actress when she walks down the red carpet. For major events, she'll wear fancy evening gowns and have her hair nicely styled. But the words Ferrera shares when she accepts an award are always heartfelt and sincere, never fake or shallow.

For example, when she won a 2007 Golden Globe award, the person Ferrera thanked the most was her mother. Ferrera thanked her for her support and guidance, saying, "Everything that I've ever accomplished in this life has been due to the strength and intelligence and will you gave to me, Mommy." Now that's keeping it real.

Ferrera's actions and her words show she is a very grounded person. Her personal warmth might be unusual among

▼ *Actress Salma Hayek,* (right) *also the executive producer of* Ugly Betty, *said of Ferrera: "I knew the minute I saw her that she was a superstar."*

celebrities with her level of fame. She values family and education, and she relates to women and Latinos on a very basic level. If she weren't an actress, she has said that she would be a teacher.

STAYING TRUE TO HERSELF

Ferrera is grateful for the opportunities she has had. She has had the luxury to be selective about the acting projects she works on. She accepts roles that allow her to express her values. She wants her work to have a positive effect on viewers. She has said of her character on *Ugly Betty*, "It's so reassuring to have a woman heroine who triumphs with more than just what she has on the outside . . . who has more to offer the world than just a pretty picture. To me, the tragedy about this whole image-obsessed society is that young girls get so caught up in just achieving that they forget to realize that they have so much more to offer the world."

Fellow actors, directors, and producers admire Ferrera for her intelligence and maturity. As an actress, she has been praised for her charm and enthusiasm for her roles. In fact, Salma Hayek said that Ferrera is "one of the most charismatic people I've ever met." She is both energetic and positive— a great combination for an actress. People also love Ferrera for her genuineness. She doesn't have to fake anything. And she doesn't.

LEARNING TO LOVE HERSELF

Think being a successful actress means having a perfect life? Think again. As a Latina growing up in a mostly white area, Ferrera struggled to fit in. "As early as second grade I remember feeling really different and isolated," she said in an interview with *W* magazine. "I had the hugest crush on a boy, and my best friend had a crush on him too. One day he said to me, 'I like your best friend more because she's paler and she has freckles.' And it was right then that I began to feel like, 'Oh wow, I'm different.'"

That feeling didn't go away even after she started acting. While she had a ton of fun filming *Gotta Kick It Up!* for the Disney Channel, it also was a bit of a letdown. "I just felt really empty," she told *W*. "I had achieved my dream, and it wasn't totally fulfilling. I still had school problems, and I still had boy problems. My life was still my life. I guess I had been waiting to be turned into a swan."

It wasn't until recently that she became more comfortable in her own skin. "Happiness is something that you have to decide to have in your life," she says she finally figured out.

"No amount of accolades [praise] can make you a happy person, and learning that as young as I did was a gift."

▶ *Ferrera has been praised for her energy and charm.*

Ferrera has been called a role model for girls for a number of reasons. Ferrera followed her dream of becoming an actress. She did whatever she needed to do to make her dream come true. That meant working in a restaurant to earn money for acting classes and taking the city bus to tryouts. She worked hard for her success. And she encourages people everywhere to follow their own dreams, no matter how unreachable they may seem.

America Ferrera tearfully thanked her mother when she won a ▶ Golden Globe award in 2007 for her work on Ugly Betty.

Awards and Recognition

Real Women Have Curves

- Nominated for an Independent Spirit Award for Best Debut Performance, 2003
- Nominated for Young Artist Award for Best Performance in a Feature Film by a Leading Young Actress, 2003
- Won Special Jury Prize for Best Actress at the Sundance Film Festival, 2002

Sisterhood of the Traveling Pants

- Won an Imagen Award for Best Actress, 2006
- Nominated for a Satellite Award for Outstanding Actress in a Supporting Role (Comedy or Musical), 2006
- Nominated for an ALMA Award for Outstanding Actress in a Motion Picture, 2006
- Nominated for a Teen Choice Award for Choice Movie Hissy Fit and Movie Breakout Performance, 2005

Ugly Betty

- Won a National Association for the Advancement of Colored People (NAACP) Image Award for Outstanding Actress in a Comedy Series, 2008
- Won a Satellite Award for Best Actress in a Series (Comedy or Musical), 2007
- Won an Imagen Award for Best Television Actress, 2007
- Won an Imagen Award for Creative Achievement, 2007

- Won a Golden Globe Award for Best Performance by an Actress in a Television Series (Musical or Comedy), 2007
- Won a Primetime Emmy for Outstanding Lead Actress in a Comedy Series, 2007
- Won an ALMA Award for Outstanding Actress in a Television Series, Mini-Series, or Television Movie, 2007
- Won a Screen Actors Guild (SAG) Award for Outstanding Performance by a Female Actor in a Television Comedy Series, 2006
- Nominated for a SAG Award for Outstanding Performance by a Female Actor in a Television Comedy Series, 2008
- Nominated for a SAG Award for Outstanding Performance by an Ensemble Cast in a Comedy Series, 2007 and 2008
- Nominated for an NAACP Image Award for Outstanding Actress in a Comedy Series, 2007
- Nominated for a Television Critics Association Award for Individual Achievement in Comedy, 2007
- Nominated for a Teen Choice Award for TV Actress in a Comedy, 2007
- Nominated for a Satellite Award for Best Actress in a Series (Comedy or Musical), 2006

Other

- Named one of fifteen most influential Hispanics in the United States by *People en Español*, 2008
- Named Hispanic Woman of the Year by *Billboard* and *Hollywood Reporter*, 2007
- Named Top Artist and Entertainer in *TIME* magazine's Top 100 Most Influential People in the World, 2007
- Won Movieline Breakthrough Award, 2005

Timeline

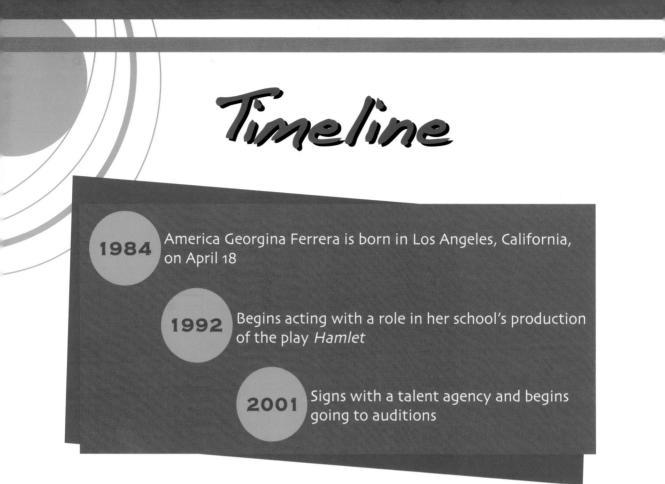

1984 America Georgina Ferrera is born in Los Angeles, California, on April 18

1992 Begins acting with a role in her school's production of the play *Hamlet*

2001 Signs with a talent agency and begins going to auditions

2002 Gets her first major acting role in July when she gets a part in Disney's TV movie *Gotta Kick It Up!*

2002 Performs in her film debut *Real Women Have Curves*

2005 Appears in *The Sisterhood of the Traveling Pants*

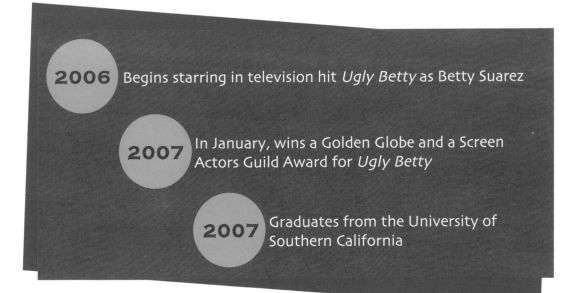

2006 Begins starring in television hit *Ugly Betty* as Betty Suarez

2007 In January, wins a Golden Globe and a Screen Actors Guild Award for *Ugly Betty*

2007 Graduates from the University of Southern California

2007 Named a top entertainer in *TIME* magazine's list of 100 Most Influential People in the World

2007 Receives an Emmy award for Best Actress in a Comedy

2008 Appears in *The Sisterhood of the Traveling Pants 2*

Further Info

BOOKS

Declare Yourself. Speak. Connect. Act. Vote. More than 50 Celebrated Americans Tell You Why. Introduction by America Ferrera. New York: Harper Collins, 2008.

Donahue, Ann. *Ugly Betty: The Book.* New York: Hyperion, 2008.

Norwich, Grace. *America the Beautiful: An Unauthorized Biography.* New York: Price Stearn Sloan, 2007.

DVDs

The Sisterhood of the Traveling Pants. Warner Home Video, 2005.

Ugly Betty—The Complete First Season. Buena Vista Home Entertainment, 2007.

INTERNET ADDRESSES

The Internet Movie Database: America Ferrera
http://www.imdb.com/name/nm1065229

Ugly Betty
http://abc.go.com/primetime/uglybetty

Glossary

audition—Short performance that tests an entertainer's abilities.

charismatic—Fascinating, charming, or appealing.

charity—An organization that raises money to help people in need.

citizenship—The rights, privileges, and duties that come with being a citizen of a certain country.

heroine—The main female character in a book, play, movie, or other kind of story.

immigrate—To move from one country to another to live there permanently.

Latina—A woman or girl from Latin America who lives in the United States.

network—A radio or television company that produces programs to broadcast.

nominate—To select for the chance to win a prize, award, or election.

stereotype—An overly simple picture of a person, group, or thing that leads to a prejudiced attitude.

Index